NO GRIER, NO GAME

NO GRIER, NO GAME

How Bobby Grier and the Sugar Bowl Showdown Changed American Sports History

Rob and Camille Grier

©2025 All Rights Reserved. No portion of this book may be reproduced, stored in a retrieval system, or transmitted in any form or by any means—electronic, mechanical, photocopy, recording, scanning, or other—except for brief quotations in critical reviews or articles without the prior permission of the author.

Published by Game Changer Publishing

Paperback ISBN: 978-1-969372-45-2

Hardcover ISBN: 978-1-969372-46-9

Digital ISBN: 978-1-969372-47-6

www.GameChangerPublishing.com

READ THIS FIRST

Just to say thanks for buying and reading *No Grier, No Game*.
Let's connect!
Scan the QR Code Here:

NO GRIER, NO GAME

HOW BOBBY GRIER AND THE SUGAR BOWL SHOWDOWN
CHANGED AMERICAN SPORTS HISTORY

ROB AND CAMILLE GRIER

FOREWORD

The 1956 Sugar Bowl holds a unique place in college football history. It was a game that pitted the University of Pittsburgh against Georgia Tech at a time when the nation was deeply divided over the issue of race. What might have been remembered simply as a hard-fought contest instead became a milestone in the struggle for equality, as Bobby Grier took the field in the first integrated football game in the history of the Deep South.

From his dorm room at Georgia Tech, my father, Wade Mitchell, watched students march to the governor's mansion in protest of political efforts to cancel the game. He witnessed firsthand how the controversy spilled beyond the field and into the very fabric of Atlanta. Yet despite the storm around them, my father and his teammates, along with coach Bobby Dodd, stood firm, honoring the game of football and respecting the man who would forever change its future.

FOREWORD

As my father later recalled: "I greatly admired Bobby's courage during that time and also the way our coach, Bobby Dodd, and my teammates stood firm against the political efforts to stop us from playing that game. There was a lot of pressure on Bobby, but he remained true to his values, and I hope that his legacy can be shared more widely through this book." Though my father and Bobby had not seen each other since 1956, their bond endured across decades. Through interviews and conversations with the media that would invariably arise with every anniversary of the game, they developed a deep respect and understanding of each other. Over sixty-five years later, when they finally reunited at Georgia Tech in July 2022, it was as if two old friends were meeting again, sharing memories, laughter, and the profound experience of having witnessed history together.

I have had the privilege of getting to know Bobby's son, Rob Grier, personally. In him, I see the same strength, courage, and integrity that defined his father. Together with his daughter, Camille, they bring this biography to life, blending family memories with historical perspective and ensuring that Bobby's story continues to inspire others to challenge the established norms. Rob and Camille's book squarely places their father's and grandfather's legacy in the greater context of the civil rights unrest in the South at the time and emphasizes Bobby's courage in challenging entrenched racial barriers and opening doors for future generations of Black athletes. Rob and Camille's tribute to Bobby is a testament to the power of standing firm in the face of pressure and to the enduring legacy one individual can leave for families, communities, and a nation.

FOREWORD

While this is a book about Bobby's incredible life and the tumultuous period leading up to the game that would change the trajectory of college sports forever, it also goes beyond the football field to illuminate other remarkable aspects of Bobby's life. This is more than a sports story; it is an American story. As President of the Georgia Trust for Historic Preservation, I spend much of my life working to honor the past and safeguard its lessons. In Bobby Grier's journey, and in the voices of Rob and Camille who carry it forward, we find a history worth remembering, celebrating, and referencing as a learning point. It is my privilege to recommend this book to you. I believe it will deepen your understanding of Bobby Grier's extraordinary life and inspire us all to continue the work of breaking racial barriers wherever they exist.

W. Wright Mitchell
September 9, 2025
Atlanta, Georgia

CONTENTS

Introduction	xiii
1. A Star on the Rise in a Divided America	1
2. Number 38 Against the Odds	15
3. While the Governor Hunted Quail	21
4. When Courage Sat in Uniform	35
5. One Yard from History	47
6. Legacy in Motion	57
7. The Next Field	69
8. The Torch and the Tunnel	79
Conclusion	91

INTRODUCTION

Massillon, Ohio, the next-door neighbor to Canton, is a football mecca where the heartbeat of the town pulses through the stadium lights on Friday nights. The crowd's roar, the clang of marching band cymbals, the scent of sweat and fresh-cut grass—it is a sacred ritual. In this small, tight-knit community of around 30,000, babies are not just born, they are inducted. Every newborn boy receives a miniature Massillon Tigers football in his crib, a ritual binding families into a lineage of grit, loyalty, and pride. It's a place where football is more than a sport; it's identity, belonging, and the promise of a shared dream. The wholehearted belief that sports can change the world is consistent throughout the town.

For my father, Bobby Grier, football became more than just a ritual. Football became a prophecy. My father is the man who, in 1956, on his twenty-third birthday, walked onto a football field in

INTRODUCTION

New Orleans and into the pages of American history. To the world, he was the first Black player to break the color barrier in the Sugar Bowl, a quiet giant whose courage forced a segregated South to face its reflection. To me, he was simply Dad. A man of faith, discipline, and humility, who never asked to be a symbol, but lived as one every day. When Bobby joined the Massillon Tigers in 1949, then coach Chuck Mather saw something in him early on: calm strength, powerful legs, and an almost eerie stillness under pressure. However, my dad's story was never just about football.

Picture America in the 1940s—at war abroad and at war with itself at home. Massillon was progressive for its time, having integrated its schools long before *Brown v. Board of Education*. Even so, invisible lines still carved up neighborhoods, schools, and opportunities. Black families, like my father's, lived under the ever-present weight of coded stares, quiet exclusion, and unwritten rules. Despite Massillon's football success, my father and his Black teammates were not shielded from the division that afflicted the country. Black players had to be twice as good just to be seen as equals. Equipment access, coaching focus, and even media coverage reflected America's deeper inequities. Outside the stadium gates, my father faced an even harsher reality. Restaurants refused service to Black people. Movie theaters had separate entrances, and there were "white" and "colored" water fountains. Nevertheless, my dad carried himself with a regal calm, formed by faith, family, and Massillon's unrelenting expectations. He was not loud; he moved with a quiet strength. He simply ran faster, blocked harder, and

INTRODUCTION

stayed later. His focus was on the football field, where he shone like a star.

As Bobby's son, I did not just hear these stories; I lived them. I watched how he treated every stranger with kindness and how he carried burdens without complaint. For years, I carried my father's story in pieces: the way teammates remembered his calm strength, the way my grandmother reminded him that dignity could be louder than protest, the way a single game revealed the contradictions of a nation torn between tradition and progress. Only as I grew older, raising my own daughter, Camille, did I realize this story is not just our family's; it belongs to America. So, I'm here to share it as a son, a father, and now, a storyteller. My life has not only been shaped by my father's quiet storm, but by the responsibility of carrying forward a legacy that is bigger than one man, one family, or one game.

Since my dad passed away in 2024, Camille and I have been reflecting on his life. This story, our family's story, is not just about football. It's about courage, resilience, and legacy. Bobby Grier did not just play through history; he moved it. And his time in Massillon? That was the forge. The fire that shaped the steel. The catalyst that spurred his greatness. He did not know it yet, but Dad's cleats were leading him into a collision with American history, one that would echo from the Sugar Bowl to the Supreme Court, and challenge the soul of a segregated nation. Camille and I wrote this book together because history should never gather dust; it should breathe, inspire, and connect generations.

Writer and philosopher George Santayana once said, "Those who cannot remember the past are condemned to repeat it." In a

INTRODUCTION

world that feels fractured, distracted, and divided, sport still speaks a common language. My father's story is not just an American football story; it is a universal story of resilience, courage, and unity that can guide us through today's cultural divides.

This book is for anyone who has ever felt unseen, underestimated, or like an underdog. This is for people who are chasing more than statistics. For families seeking hope. For leaders seeking to understand what true courage and resilience look like when the lights are brightest and the pressure is heaviest. For every reader who longs to believe that one person's choices can ripple outward and change the world. I carry not only the eyewitness perspective of the son of a legend, but also the responsibility of a family legacy. Camille and I have delved into archives, sat with teammates now in their nineties, and pieced together our story with love, research, and lived experience.

In this book, you will encounter Bobby Grier not as a footnote in sports history, but as a mirror for your own life. You will see how his "currency of courage" is as relevant now as it was in 1956. My goal in telling my father's story is that you will come away with lessons in perseverance, leadership, legacy, and unity that can shape how you live, lead, and love. As you read this book, you will see reflection questions at the end of each chapter that encourage you to consider how Bobby's story relates to your own life as well as current events, and how you, too, can make a difference.

I hope that this book reminds you that courage does not always roar; sometimes it walks quietly onto a field, carrying nothing but dignity and determination. I hope that you will feel

INTRODUCTION

empowered to face your own invisible barriers and to see that legacy is not measured by trophies or headlines, but by the lives you touch. From the fields of grit and brotherhood to the roar of the Sugar Bowl, Bobby's journey is more than history. It is a call to remember that we are *all* part of the same story: one of courage, unity, and legacy.

CHAPTER 1
A STAR ON THE RISE IN A DIVIDED AMERICA

Long before Bobby wore a jersey or laced up his cleats beneath the Massillon stadium lights, his story began with loss and legacy. At three months old, he lost his father, John Henry Lowry, a man the community affectionately called "Big Jenny." Bobby's mother (and my grandmother), Mary, was Big Jenny's seamstress and had three sons by him. They never got married, but the Lowrys accepted Grandma Mary and the boys, and our families remain close. After Big Jenny's passing in 1933, Mary decided that Ray, Fred, and Bobby would carry her last name: Grier.

Big Jenny was a towering figure in both stature and spirit, a Black man who had built a life of quiet defiance in the face of segregation. He was a prolific businessman in town, owning the Vahepa Hotel, a waste collection company, the Lowry Pop Bottling Works, and a brick factory whose bricks were used to build the Massillon YMCA and Shiloh Baptist Church. He donated buildings to his community, his generosity leaving fingerprints on the very heart of the town. He was a Black millionaire in the 1930s, a living example of the American Dream, built on determination, resilience, and vision. When he died, the city flew its flag at half-mast, a rare honor for a Black man in the early 20th century. A statement that legacy can outshine prejudice, even if only for a moment.

Big Jenny's death left a silent void in the town of Massillon and in his family. Though Bobby grew up without a father, his mother and older brothers, Ray and Fred, became his steadfast pillars. They taught him that dignity could be louder than protest and that the way he walked through the world would one day open doors for others. Bobby's mother was a rock of grace and grit, and she raised him with the armor of spirituality.

John Henry "Big Jenny" Lowry

Her faith was unshakeable, her wisdom deep and everlasting, and her homemade recipes mouthwatering. Her voice echoed in his ears as he ran sprints and ducked under tackles: "You are not just playing for yourself. You play for the whole town."

In their home, the smell of cornbread, squirrel soup, and Sunday roasts mixed with the hum of gospel hymns. My dad and his brothers would catch possums, rabbits, and squirrels so that their mother could turn them into delicacies. Bobby learned hard work from his brothers. They did not just raise him; they forged him to live with humility, discipline, and grace under pressure. They taught him that true strength was not in what the world gave you, but in how you carried yourself when the world looked away.

Outside the united walls of Massillon, America from the 1910s to the 1940s was raw, divided, and unforgiving. Massacres, where white mobs would go into Black towns, burn homes and businesses, and murder without a conscience or consequences, continued to terrorize people. From the Washington and Chicago Race Riots to the Elaine Massacre in Arkansas (all in 1919), to the Tulsa Race Massacre in 1921, to the Rosewood Massacre in 1923, and to the Detroit Race Riot of 1943, people of color were seen as animals who needed to be hunted and treated worse than dogs. They were dragged around town by a rope, lynched, and set on fire as gleeful onlookers took pictures or cut off body parts from the mutilated body to share with family and friends.

Bobby's own family, cousins of Bobby's mother, had a thriving shoe business in Tulsa until they were murdered, and the entire town was burned to the ground. The Griers had a lot of family in the South—Alabama, Georgia, and South Carolina. Mary moved from Alabama to Massillon, seeking a better chance of survival in the North.

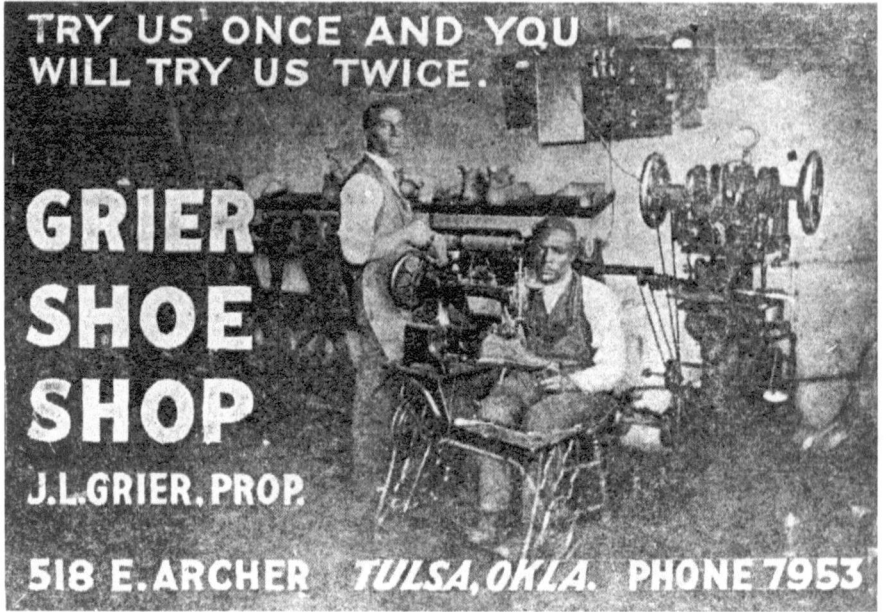

Grier Family Shoe Shop promotional poster, before the Tulsa Race Massacre

For young Black men, life was a quiet negotiation with danger. A wrong look, being in the wrong place, or receiving the wrong kind of attention could cost you your life. Lynchings and disappearances were whispered reminders that freedom was conditional according to the color of your skin. In 1930, J. Thomas Shipp and Abram S. Smith became prime examples of how simple it could be to be killed by mobs of people who hate you solely for your skin color. The news and the iconic photo (following) spread across the country and the world. Even as World War II would pull the nation together abroad, the war for dignity at home remained unrelenting.

J. Thomas Shipp and Abraham S. Smith hanged from a tree in front of a crowd, August 7th, 1930, Marion, Indiana

Bobby grew up in that tension, learning to move quietly, to let his actions speak louder than his words. He watched his mother, brothers, neighbors, and church elders measure every step, knowing that survival depended as much on restraint as it did on resilience. And deep down, he also felt the influence of his late father's success and hard work. Bobby's neighbor and best friend growing up, Alex Paris, shared his same path, literally, from kindergarten through twelfth grade. They walked to school together through snowfalls and sunny mornings, their shoes pounding the same sidewalks, their futures unknowingly intertwining. The two even played basketball together at Jones Middle School. A white boy and a Black boy, their friendship embodied how Massillon quietly defied racial barriers while building champions on and off the field. Alex later became superintendent of Massillon schools. He was not only a friend but a steady presence in Bobby's life, the kind who shows up when there is no one watching. The kind of friend who reminds you who you are when the world forgets. It was these unseen moments—backyard football, long walks to and from school, fishing, exploring, and quiet conversation—that built Dad's resilience. His brotherhood gave Dad a tribe, one where skin color was invisible, before he ever wore a jersey. This community, his family and friends, was the quiet training ground for a life that would demand both courage and calculation.

Jones Middle School basketball team, Bobby Grier (number 46, back row, third from right), Alex Paris (number 43, front row, second from left)

By the late 1940s, Dad's talent on the field began to outshine the shadows. Massillon, Ohio, with its storied football tradition, became his first stage. The Massillon Tigers were not just a team; they were a way of life. Gritty, relentless, and proud, Massillon birthed legends. It has produced over one hundred NFL players and was coached at one point by the infamous Paul Brown. Brown became the architect of modern football—co-founder, first coach, and namesake of the Cleveland Browns, and later, co-founder of the Cincinnati Bengals. Across town sits Canton, where the Pro Football Hall of Fame anchors the game's history and where generations of rivalry with the Massillon Tigers have shaped both towns since the late 1800s. The battles between Massillon and Canton McKinley have long been more than games; they were sermons, civic pride, and proving grounds where careers were made and legacies tested.

Out of this crucible emerged my father, Bobby Grier. His story echoed the same grit that built steel, the same belief in progress that fueled his father's success, and the same pursuit of excellence that defined Massillon football. As a teenager, Dad's plays lit up the field, but it was his persistence that stayed with people. In one game, a near loss turned into a comeback as Bobby delivered a bone-jarring hit on defense. No chest pounding, no showboating, no dancing, just a hand up to the opponent and a rushed hustle back to the huddle. It flipped the momentum. Dad's teammates could feel it, his coaches could not stop talking about it, and his opponents would never forget it.

Bobby's varsity journey began in the fall of 1949. He laced up his cleats, slipped on jersey number 48, and stepped onto the sacred grass of Tiger Stadium, a teenager carrying the weight of a town obsessed with winning. Bobby was talented, but he didn't succeed alone. His family was behind him one hundred percent. Literally, they were in the stands cheering him on; figuratively, they were with him on the field, in the locker room, and on every walk to school that shaped the man he would become. During the 1949 season, his older brother Fred, number 63, lined up in the Tigers' black and orange, both a teammate and a quiet rival. They pushed each other harder, ran drills longer, and held one another to a standard that only blood could understand. The kind of sibling fire that sharpens iron with iron.

Massillon 1949 championship team, Bobby Grier (number 48, third row, fifth from right), and Fred Grier (number 63, bottom row, far right)

With an energy matching the beat of the drumline pulsing throughout the stadium, Bobby fought alongside his teammates through a season of grit and heartbreak. That year, the Massillon Tigers clawed their way to a near-perfect record, even beating arch-rival Canton McKinley. Then, one game changed everything. The Mansfield Tygers, another rival. Mansfield - 16; Massillon - 12. A single loss that left the town stunned and the players aching. The Ohio polls ranked Massillon number one that year, but they were not crowned champions. It was a strange kind of honor, victory without a trophy, recognition without the ring. For my dad, it was not just the scoreboard that hurt; it was the silent question it left behind: Was "almost" ever good enough? While he didn't know the answer, the fire of determination was his life. He was not finished.

In 1950, Dad traded jersey number 48 for number 58, and heartbreak for destiny. Dad's work ethic did not need a spotlight; it cast its own. While his teammates joked around, Dad showed up to practice early. While everyone celebrated the wins, Dad studied films from previous games. Yes, they did have game films in 1950! Coaches noticed his determination, and Bobby became a leader whom his teammates looked up to.

Under crisp autumn skies and the roar of packed stands, the Massillon Tigers rebounded with purpose. They not only won their games; they dominated the 1950 season. The Tigers made a statement that year with a 10-0 record. They were Ohio state champions and national high school champions. For Bobby, it was not the scoreboard that mattered most; it was the soul behind the stats. Every tackle, every yard, every silent prayer in the locker room was part of a bigger story: redemption.

Massillon 1950 state and national champions, Bobby Grier (number 58, third row, right of center)

The sting of the previous year's "almost" had been transformed into a brotherhood-driven triumph that electrified the town and stamped a legacy on Bobby's name. The victory rang through the community like a hymn: When one rises, we all rise. For my dad, this was just the beginning. A proving ground of purpose. A season that proclaimed: "You were made for more than this field." The young man who once questioned if "almost" was enough had now led a team straight to the top.

By the end of the 1950 season, Bobby was not just respected; he was counted on. He became a north star in cleats. Beneath the cheers and chalkboards, deeper lessons were forming. Courage, leadership, discipline, humility. My father lived these traits every single day of his life. Even when the odds tilted out of his favor and the whispers of others tried to define him, he answered with action, not argument.

For Bobby, those years between the goalposts at Massillon Washington High School were not just about plays or points. They were about proving your worth in a town where the scoreboard measured more than the game. Each snap of the ball carried the weight of legacy and a silent battle for belonging. Every play was a heartbeat in the town's collective chest. With every yard gained, the beating of Bobby's heart as he rushed down the field echoed louder than the cheers in the stands. The excitement was palpable. It was in this cauldron of pressure and pride that Bobby stood out, not with bravado, but with poise and focus. He was a young man becoming a compass for something bigger than football.

Dad's every action on the field carved his place in a story that, for some, was never written to include him: a young Black man playing football in the 1950s. Bobby succeeded against all odds. He kept showing up, and he wrote his own story. Why? Because in a divided America—even in a football town that prided itself on unity—being a Black athlete meant you had to win twice: on the field and in life. My father was ready for both.

In today's world, college athletes are rewarded for their name, image, and likeness (NIL), with little consideration for their own legacy. They sign endorsement deals, film commercials, and collect checks that change their lives before their first professional snap. Bobby had to prove himself in a much different way than today's athletes. When Division I recruiters came calling—Notre Dame, Ohio State, Nebraska, Michigan, Syracuse—one team stood out in particular for Bobby. The University of Pittsburgh saw more than a running back; they saw a young man whose integrity, humility, and quiet power could carry a team and, unknowingly, a nation.

A young Black man from Ohio was about to enter a stage built for giants. And he would hold his own. His currency was courage, and his endorsement was risk itself. He risked ridicule, exclusion, even his own safety, for the right to belong on that field. Despite selective beliefs, the parallels between now and then are unavoidable. Today, the stadiums are bigger, the cameras sharper, and the paydays larger. But our country still wrestles with extreme violence and political and social division. We scroll through polarized feeds, where neighbors feel like strangers and opinions are weaponized. Politics has become a sport, and social media has drawn new color lines of tribe, ideology, and identity.

Bobby's story reminds us that while the field has changed, the battle for character, unity, and courage is timeless. His footsteps on the grass of the 1950s echo into the turf of today, an encouragement to every athlete and every American: Excellence can bridge divides, if we allow it. And Bobby? He could not yet know that the next steps he took would carry him into the national spotlight. Not just to break records, but to break barriers the nation was not ready to face. His cleats would carve through more than mud; they would cut into the conscience of America and leave marks that would never fade.

REFLECTION QUESTIONS:

1. Have you ever faced unspoken or invisible barriers? If so, how did you break barriers?
2. How do the people, environments, and experiences that have shaped you—like those that shaped Bobby's character—influence your values, sense of identity, and purpose?
3. What does Bobby's quiet strength teach you about leading without needing the spotlight? Who in your life has helped you to lead by example rather than words?
4. What lessons can modern athletes and leaders learn from Bobby's "currency of courage" compared to today's NIL era?
5. How does Bobby's upbringing in an era of silent strength mirror the quiet battles we face in today's divided society?
6. How can Bobby's story inspire conversations about unity over division in sports, communities, and the nation at large?

CHAPTER 2
NUMBER 38 AGAINST THE ODDS

In the fall of 1952, Bobby officially stepped onto the University of Pittsburgh's football field, not just as a Panther, but as a symbol of possibility.

My father donned jersey number 38; little did he know that this number would be synonymous with the name "Bobby Grier" for generations to come. Upon his shoulders, he carried the weight of generations. He carried unspoken prayers whispered in church pews and around kitchen tables by families who longed to see a young Black man break through the barriers that had hemmed them in for decades. In that era, football was not just a game. Football was a mirror, reflecting the nation's deep divides, lines of scrimmage on the field, and invisible lines of prejudice beyond it.

While Bobby's team in high school was integrated, he was the only Black player on the Pitt Panthers team. A living experiment in progress and pressure, he could not simply play the game he loved; he had to play it perfectly. A single fumble would echo louder than a touchdown. A missed block would feed the whispered prejudice of those waiting for him to fail. Every game was a test of skill, yes, but more so of endurance, grace, and restraint. No excuses, no room for error.

Life on the road carried a different kind of scoreboard. In 1950s America, hotels and restaurants were often divided by unspoken rules. Even in the North, doors did not always open equally. At the time, there were freshmen-only football teams, and one trip that the Pitt Panther freshmen team took to Annapolis, Maryland, to face the Naval Academy stands out as a prime example of the trials my father endured. The night before the game, the team went to see a movie. Bobby was stopped at the door. The theater was for "whites only." While his teammates took their seats inside, Dad was quietly directed to a segregated theater down the street. He did not argue; he did not complain. He just left. The silence of that night was a heavy reminder of where the country stood on segregation. Years later, some of Dad's teammates admitted they should have left with him. They should have said something, stood in solidarity with my dad. That moment revealed the courage that many lacked to stand up for what was right and speak out against injustice.

Dad's journey was a collision of grit and grace, a masterclass in silent leadership. He lived what modern coaches and champions preach: No regrets. Leave it all on the field. He absorbed every hit, every slight, and every unspoken expectation with a calm dignity that became his armor. The invisible lines that my father crossed in 1952, when he started as a freshman football player at Pitt, still echo, though they have shifted into new shapes. His story reminds us that true leadership does not always roar; it endures, unbroken and unshaken, in the face of adversity.

The 1955 season began like a drumbeat, steady and unrelenting: Every snap, every block, every tackle marked time against a country on the edge of transformation. Bobby Grier stepped into that season as more than a Pitt Panther. He continued to wear jersey number 38 on his back, while carrying the weight of history and the silent expectations of thousands who would never step on that field.

University of Pittsburgh Panthers, varsity team, 1955, Bobby Grier (number 38, third row from bottom, second from right)

At the time, Black athletes in Division I football could be counted in dozens, not hundreds. The South remained mostly segregated. Some schools even refused to play if a Black athlete took the field. Even in the North, integration was tolerated but rarely embraced. Every first, second, and third down was a quiet negotiation with history. Bobby played with bruised knuckles and a steady heartbeat. His body absorbed the violence of the game. His presence absorbed the weight of a movement still finding its voice. On the football field, Bobby was both a tank and a tactician. Being a fullback on offense, he lowered his shoulders into defensive walls. On defense as a linebacker, he diagnosed plays with surgical precision.

His teammates, including Gordy Oliver, Corky Cost, Joe Walton, Bob Rosborough, and co-captain John Cenci, among others, trusted him implicitly. Together, they forged a team that could stare down anyone, including legends like Jim Brown, whom Bobby and Pitt held to just twenty-eight yards on twelve carries in a statement game, beating the mighty Syracuse. The wins continued to pile up. Syracuse fell. Pitt shut out Penn State 20–0 in "Unhappy" Valley. In the legendary backyard brawl, West Virginia, the chosen favorite for a Sugar Bowl invitation, fell 26–7 at Pitt Stadium. The Pitt Panthers finished the 1955 season 7–3, and Bobby's leadership had become about more than football; it was a quiet revolution in cleats. Leading Pittsburgh sports writer Myron Cope took a shot at The Ohio State University with the following headline:

"Notice, OSU: Pitt's 2 Top Fullbacks are Ohioans; Tom Jenkins from East Liverpool, Giving Bobby Grier from Massillon Stiff Battle"

However, outside the stadium at the University of Pittsburgh, America was on fire. While the South marched, my dad played his own protest, gaining yard after yard to plead and prove that he belonged. He didn't carry protest signs; he carried the football.

That was his form of protest. Bobby never shouted; he stared down history. His excellence was an act of resistance, as radical in its own way as Rosa Parks' quiet defiance.

As the Pitt Panthers clawed their way to national relevance, murmurs of the Sugar Bowl began to circulate. It was the pinnacle of college football. When they got the good news in November 1955, it should have felt like a triumph. Pittsburgh's invitation to one of college football's seven great national stages —the Sugar Bowl in New Orleans, Louisiana—shifted the trajectory of history. For most players, this was the dream. For Bobby, it would mean something more, a collision of sport and society under the harshest lights. Destiny and danger intertwined. History was in the making, and Bobby Grier was running directly towards it. Humble, quiet, and relentless, he was about to step into a game that would forever change college football and America itself. When the whistle blew, the world would be watching.

When segregationists in the South saw a Black man's name on the roster, letters began to fly, and threats were muttered. Behind closed doors, powerful men debated whether one Black man's presence was worth a game, a season, a title win, or the old order of the South. Simmering racial tensions ignited into a firestorm. A game became a referendum, and a young man became a symbol. The weight of history once again settled quietly onto Bobby's shoulders.

1955 University of Pittsburgh Panthers Football Team Game Results (7-3)

Game 1	**Pittsburgh**	27	California	7
Game 2	**Pittsburgh**	22	Syracuse	12
Game 3	Pittsburgh	14	**Oklahoma**	**26**
Game 4	Pittsburgh	0	**Navy**	**21**
Game 5	**Pittsburgh**	21	Nebraska	7
Game 6	**Pittsburgh**	26	Duke	7
Game 7	Pittsburgh	7	**Miami (FL)**	**21**
Game 8	**Pittsburgh**	18	Virginia	7
Game 9	**Pittsburgh**	26	West Virginia	7
Game 10	**Pittsburgh**	20	Penn State	0

REFLECTION QUESTIONS:

1. In today's still divided society, how can Bobby's story of quiet excellence and leadership inspire current athletes and leaders to use their platforms for lasting impact?
2. What parallels exist between Bobby's era of playing without safety nets and modern NIL athletes navigating fame, pressure, and social responsibility?
3. How does Bobby's experience demonstrate the intersection of athletics and civil rights, and what lessons from his approach echo in the invisible battles of today's justice movements?

CHAPTER 3
WHILE THE GOVERNOR HUNTED QUAIL

America in late 1955 was already trembling with change. In May of the previous year, the Supreme Court had issued its seismic ruling in *Brown v. Board of Education*. This unanimous decision declared separate public schools for Black and white students unconstitutional. It was more than a legal declaration; it was a line in the sand. But progress did not arrive with fanfare; it came with friction. Across America, the promise of equality was still just that, a promise. In Southern towns, school doors remained shut. Not to white children, but to the idea of integration. Governors promised "massive resistance." White Citizens' Councils sprang up like weeds, spreading venom with politeness and a legal veneer. The ink on the Brown decision had barely dried when the South began sharpening its teeth.

In August of 1955, a fourteen-year-old boy named Emmett Till stepped off a train from Chicago, visiting his cousins in the Mississippi Delta. He carried no weapon, only a photograph of his mother and the swagger of a city kid raised to believe he mattered. What followed was not just a tragedy. It was an atrocity. They said he whistled at a white woman. This accusation ended in a brutal beating. His body was found mutilated beyond recognition, bloated from the Tallahatchie River. An eye gouged out. A bullet in his skull. A fan tied around his neck like barbed wire, as if someone wanted to make sure he never floated again.

Article leading up to the Emmett Till murder trial, September 19, 1955

His mother, Mamie Till-Mobley, made the world look. She demanded an open casket. *Jet* Magazine printed the photo. The world saw Emmett's face, or rather, what was left of it, and felt America's soul tear at the seams. Black America could never unsee it. White America could no longer pretend. The grotesque truth of the country's darker side burned into people's conscience like a brand.

Then, on December 1st, 1955, in Montgomery, Alabama, Rosa Parks refused to give up her bus seat, sparking the Montgomery Bus Boycott. She was not just tired from a day's work. She was exhausted by a country that kept sitting on its conscience. Leaders like a young Martin Luther King Jr. took to pulpits with fire in their voices. The civil rights movement, once a quiet storm, now thundered across the land. Across the South, white resistance hardened as Black courage rose. While the South was ablaze, up North in steel towns along the Monongahela River, like Pittsburgh, Black athletes were pushing through a different kind of resistance. Not the overt, mob-fueled violence of southern states, but the institutionalized friction of northern respectability politics. Integration existed on paper, but barriers were invisible, coded, polite, and just as real.

The announcement that the University of Pittsburgh would accept an invitation to the Sugar Bowl set off a political wildfire. Not because of their record, nor because of the matchup. Solely because of one man, Bobby, the lone Black player on Pitt's roster. New Orleans was a city known for gumbo, jazz, and segregation, where its charm and its cruelty co-existed in plain sight. Deep in the segregated South, Jim Crow still ruled. This system of laws and customs divided schools, restaurants, water fountains, buses, and stadium seats by skin color. Black excellence was tolerated at a distance, but placing a Black athlete in a nationally celebrated Southern bowl game was considered unthinkable.

As the news broke that Bobby Grier would suit up for the Panthers, the reaction from Southern leadership came in swiftly and with venomous intent. The first strike of resistance came from Georgia's governor, Marvin Griffin, who thundered from his pulpit of power. He railed against the very idea of integration, vowing that no team from his state, especially Georgia Tech, would dare take the field against a Black player. His threats were not hollow. He hinted at slashing university funding, pulling political favors, and exacting retribution on those who disobeyed his segregationist mandate. He sent a public telegram to the Board of Regents of the University System of

Georgia on December 2nd, 1955, condemning Bobby's participation:

> *"I urge you most emphatically to take every step to prevent Georgia Tech from being a party to such a contest involving interracial competition,"* Griffin declared in a telegram to the Board of Regents. *"The South stands at Armageddon. The battle is joined for the survival of our way of life. We cannot make the slightest concession to the enemy in this dark and lamentable hour of struggle. If we continue to make these concessions, our children will be little better than mulattoes. There is no more difference in compromising integrity of race on the playing field than in doing so in the classrooms. One break in the dike and the relentless seas will rush in and destroy us."*

These words were a threat draped in official authority, echoing decades of intimidation. Griffin's position was emblematic of the entrenched segregationist attitudes that dominated Southern politics. He was a staunch defender of Jim Crow, and he would later become infamous as the running mate for George Wallace, a presidential candidate notorious for his vehement opposition to integration and friendship with the Ku Klux Klan. Some whispered about Griffin's alignment with white supremacist groups. Others feared the real danger would come from the crowds, the streets, or the quiet violence that always seemed to follow moments like this. Bobby was no longer just a football player. He was a litmus test.

Georgia Tech president Blake Van Leer and legendary football head coach Bobby Dodd faced enormous pressure. To forfeit would appease the governor but betray the principles of sport. To play without Bobby would shame the university and compromise the integrity of the game. Van Leer, a man of quiet steel, stood firm: "We signed the contract. We will play. If you prevent us from playing in the Sugar Bowl, you will have to find another damn President to run this institution." No apologies or retractions. Later, Van Leer became well known as the "Damn President." Bobby Dodd backed him, and so did his players.

Bobby Dodd was born Robert Lee "Bobby" Dodd in Virginia in 1908, named by his father after Confederate General Robert E. Lee. While official programs of the era occasionally highlighted his full name, historical accounts show that Dodd himself was not likened to Lee in character or leadership. In fact, the resemblance ended with the name. Known as "The Whistle" for his quiet, understated style, Dodd was soft-spoken and player-focused, valuing the health and well-being of his athletes above winning at all costs. In the cultural stage of Southern football, where symbolism carried weight and names could evoke identity and tradition, the presence of a coach named after Robert E. Lee naturally echoed the South's pride in its past. Yet Dodd's actions would ultimately chart a very different course.

That forward-thinking leadership became clear in 1956, when his team faced the University of Pittsburgh in the Sugar Bowl. At a time when segregationist politicians in Georgia threatened to block the game because Pitt had a Black player, Dodd stood with Georgia Tech's president in insisting the game proceed, even as the president offered to resign in protest. That decision helped crack open the door of integration in Southern college football. Later, as Georgia Tech's athletic director, Dodd played a key role in recruiting Eddie McAshan, the school's first Black quarterback, in 1969. Far from embodying the region's defiance against civil rights, Bobby Dodd's legacy is one of integrity, quiet courage, and progress; a shining star who helped lead college football through a time of enormous change.

With Van Leer, Dodd, and the Tech football team all taking a stand, the students rose up. Griffin's bark had ignited something he had not anticipated: a rebellion.

Bobby Dodd from 1963 *Blueprint* magazine

Georgia Tech students and players, to their credit, erupted like hot lava and set out to destroy anything in their path to play this game. Two thousand students stormed Five Points, a neighborhood in the heart of downtown Atlanta. Little Five Points is a distinct neighborhood historically known for its bohemian vibe, independent businesses, and vibrant arts scene, located east of downtown. Beyond Five Points, the rebellious rioters descended upon the State Capitol. They refused to let the governor rewrite the script of sports and history. Rioters tore down the state flag. Protest signs clashed with Jim Crow's ideologies. Multiple effigies of Governor Griffin were hoisted high, then set aflame, their charred remains a symbol of youth no longer willing to be silent.

They defaced statues of Confederate heroes with signs that read "We Play Ball!," "SUGAR BOWL," "To Hell with Griffin," "We hope all the gov's children are Black," and "We hate people who hate niggers."

New York Herald Tribune, 1955

Georgia Tech protests, 1955

Rioters protesting Governor Griffin, 1955

Georgia Tech Protestors hanging Governor Griffin in effigy, 1955

College students across several Georgia universities joined the chorus, some chanting for the game, others for justice—most for both. Still, the firestorm did not end there.

After descending upon the State Capitol, the mob broke through the Georgia Bureau of Investigations (GBI) barricades and breached the State Capitol, causing havoc, overturning desks and trash cans. The rage-filled students next headed for the governor's mansion. Governor Griffin was nowhere to be found. He was hiding in the woods hunting quail. While his city rioted, and his people marched and chanted his name in jeers across the Georgia Tech campus, Griffin was "down South," shotgun in hand, aiming at birds instead of facing the moral reckoning exploding in his own capital.

This headline written by William A. Fowlkes said it all:

"Ga. Governor Hunts Quail As Tech's Students Riot"

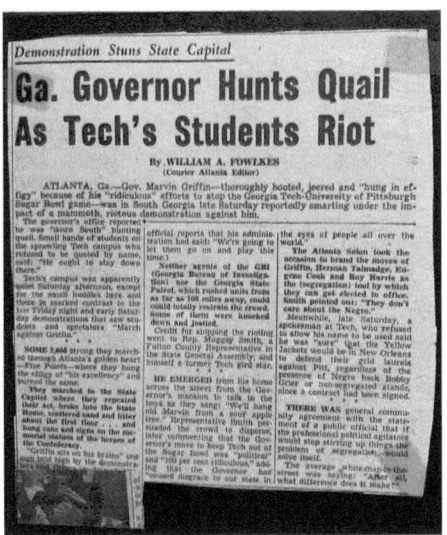

Article by William A. Fowlkes, Courier Atlanta Editor

It read like satire, and it played like prophecy.

Somewhere deep in the brush, as Griffin leveled his sights on game birds, history was leveling as he put out a statement, "declaring the executive mansion is under a state of siege." For the next three days, the governor's mansion was placed under a twenty-four-hour guard.

New York Herald Tribune, 1955

The *New York Herald Tribune* chronicled the riots:

"Some 2,000 angry students tried to storm the Governor's mansion after leaving the State Capitol in shambles, but they were forced back by a cordon of hundreds of police and State Highway patrolmen. The students fought with building guards and Georgia Bureau of Investigation agents on the Capitol steps, before they marched on Governor Griffin's official residence. There, a solid line of city and county police and

troopers reinforced by detachments from seven other cities forced back the throng of shouting, placard-waving students."

Griffin's attempt to halt progress had turned him into a symbol of absurdity. As one protester's sign read: *"What difference does it make?"* This very question tore through the myth of segregation like buckshot, ripping open the truth that the world was watching, and the South could no longer hide behind its tired, old excuses.

The question was as clear as it was divisive: Should Bobby Grier play?

Atlanta still seethed with chaos, tear gas, curfews, and furious debate. The Georgia Board of Regents, in a rare break from Governor Griffin, sided with Georgia Tech's decision to play. Meanwhile, back at the Sugar Bowl Committee headquarters, the tension crackled like a downed power line. In the end, however, inclusion spoke louder than hate. The Sugar Bowl Committee also sided with unity. Bobby Grier would play in the 1956 Sugar Bowl. And Georgia and Louisiana, whether they liked it or not, had taken their first step onto the right side of history.

In that moment, Griffin became the face of a dying era of white supremacy, caught reloading while the future marched on without him. By the time the one-term governor was done hunting quail, America had already found its target. His furious attempt to block my father's participation in the Sugar Bowl was now national news, and not in the way that he had hoped. Griffin's antics had become a national embarrassment. People didn't just mock his ridiculous assertions of racial posturing and Civil War nostalgia; they pitied them.

One truth that rang out louder than the protests, the press conferences, or the posturing: Bobby is just another guy. He's a person, like anyone else. Except, of course, to Governor Griffin, who wanted Bobby to remain a symbol of why the South believes they won the Civil War. Negro athletes were excelling "on the impartial basis of ability," dominating baseball pennants, basketball champions, and boxing divisions. They had become the backbone of American sport. And yet, here stood a Governor, clinging to segregation as if it were a hunting dog refusing to heel.

Today, the irony is staggering. Over sixty percent of Division I football and NFL rosters are composed of Black athletes. The very institutions and industries that once resisted their inclusion now build empires on their brawn and brilliance. In 1956, though, that future was anything but guaranteed. It took men like Bobby Grier. It took men like Jackie Robinson and Roy Campanella. It took men like Willie O'Ree. It took headlines that stood like monuments against the tide of hate. The future needed moments like this.

And what of Pitt? What of Bobby's team? That story, their decision, their brotherhood, and their defiance mark the next layer of this history—and it changes everything.

REFLECTION QUESTIONS:

1. What does Emmett Till's story reveal about the hidden costs of being Black in America during the 1950s? How does understanding this historical context reshape how we view Bobby's courage and the emotional weight he carried?
2. In what ways can we, as humans, carry Bobby's spirit forward in today's divided world? How can individuals and institutions show up in the face of discrimination and adversity?
3. What do you take away from the difference between Van Leer's and Dodd's defiance and Griffin's noise? How might this change how you show up in the face of adversity?
4. How can understanding the Georgia Tech student uprising help us interpret today's cultural flashpoints, from the Black Lives Matter movement to social media polarization?

CHAPTER 4
WHEN COURAGE SAT IN UNIFORM

In the lead-up to the game, newspapers buzzed with opinion columns, angry letters, and political grandstanding from *The New York Times* and *The Atlanta Journal-Constitution* to *Sports Illustrated*. The *Pittsburgh Post-Gazette* chronicled the mounting tension. The articles painted Bobby not just as a running back and linebacker, but as a young man who had become a flashpoint between the old world and the new. Meanwhile, Black newspapers like the *Pittsburgh Courier* and *The Chicago Defender* wrote with clarity and conviction. Bobby was more than a player. He had become a symbol of what a new America could look like. Many of Bobby's white counterparts could never imagine what he had to overcome just to step onto the field. Hunting the ball on the football field could not compare to being hunted in your own neighborhood. Bobby was a quiet warrior advancing on segregation with nothing but dignity, cleats, and resolve.

University of Pittsburgh students in support of Bobby, 1955

Bobby had even received interest from the National Football League. This letter from the Chicago Cardinals carried a subtle promise: talent and character like his could not be ignored. It was a quiet reminder that even as the weight of history pressed on his shoulders, the world of professional football was watching.

"Dear Bob,

Our office is compiling a file on prospective players for the 1956 National Football League draft.

We would appreciate it if you would fill out the enclosed questionnaire and return it to us so that we will have the necessary information to complete your file.

Though you may be entering military service or planning some other type of activity in the near future, we would like to have this form returned.

Looking forward to hearing from you at an early date, we are,

Sincerely yours,
Chicago Cardinals Football Club
Ray Richards
Head Coach"

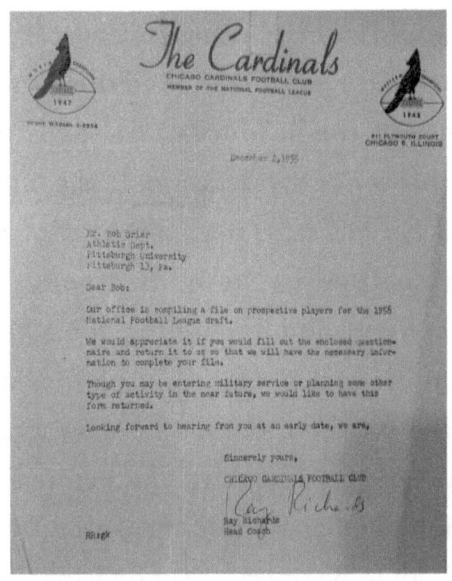

Letter to Bobby from the Chicago Cardinals, December 2, 1955

Behind the headlines, something extraordinary had unfolded. Georgia Tech was ready to play the game against Pitt and Bobby Grier. Inside Pitt's own walls, debates flared. Some university leaders feared the worst. Should they hold Bobby back? Protect him from the storm he was walking into? Or would pulling him be a betrayal louder than any cheer or boo from the stands?

In contrast to the rioting, protests, and worried questioning, the team in Pittsburgh took a quieter approach to the situation. The Pitt locker room in 1956 was sacred ground—a temple of brotherhood, sweat sacrifice, and unspoken bonds in the gritty city of steel. That frosty week in December became a courtroom for history. Coach John Michelosen, in his first season and already leading the Panthers to the prestigious Sugar Bowl, made a decision few would dare: He turned inward. He gathered the team, looked into their eyes, and handed them the moment.

"You all have seen the headlines," he said. "You know what's happening. But this is not my decision. It is yours. Whatever you decide, we stand behind it." Then, unheard of for the time, he ordered all the coaches to leave the room. They filed out, followed by Michelosen, and he shut the doors behind them. The team remained in the locker room, sitting in silence, feeling the weight of a nation on their shoulders. Co-captains John Cenci and Harold Hunter stepped forward, but before they could speak, my father rose politely. Calmly and measured. Not a victim but a man determined not to be the cause of division.

"Fellas, it's been a long season," Bobby said. "We are all banged up, tired. I want to go to New Orleans and fight with my brothers. But, if my being there costs us that chance, I'll say I am injured. You go, I'll stay."

Silence.

Then, from the back, a voice cut through: "If Bobby doesn't go, we don't go." Every hand raised. Unanimous. Fast. Fierce. A verdict not in anger, but in unity. When the coaches walked back into that locker room, they did not find a football team. They found a revolution in cleats. Pittsburgh's official stance wired to Sugar Bowl Officials and Georgia Tech was, "No Grier, No Game." They were not willing to cave under the racist pressure from the governor of Georgia. The moment that turned teammates into brothers and opponents into history was not decided in a courtroom, a governor's office, or even in the stands; it was forged behind closed doors, deep inside the locker room of the University of Pittsburgh.

No Grier. No Game.

Bobby's Pitt teammates showing their support, 1955

In that moment, football became a moral stage, and the young Pitt Panthers became actors in a play much larger than themselves. The Sugar Bowl was not only a football game. It was a line in the sand for many in the South. Dad's quiet courage, matched by the integrity of his teammates, was a message to every stadium, every classroom, and every boardroom in America. It said: Unity is the future. It will be different because we are willing to stand for it. Sportswriters across the country called it a test of courage, not for Bobby, who had never wavered, but for America itself.

My daughter, Camille, and I often talk about this moment as the soul of Dad's legacy. When the spotlight came, he did not chase it. When the pressure mounted, he did not break. He just kept showing up, letting his actions speak the truth: *I belong here.*

Later, players would call that vote one of the most emotional decisions of their lives, more intense than getting married, for some. It was the kind of decision that carves itself into a man's bones. My father fondly recalled this moment and how it brought him to tears, knowing his team stood with him. One teammate even said, "We were not just choosing to play with Bobby. We were choosing what kind of men we wanted to be. We chose unity." The 1955–56 Panthers were not solely a football team; they became a family. A sacred brotherhood forged not in the absence of adversity, but because of it.

Fast forward to today's locker rooms, where players bounce between schools, chasing NIL dollars and hoping for short-term gain while risking long-term legacy. They post highlight reels on social media, secure sponsorships, and gauge their value based on clicks and contracts. But what the 1955–56 Panthers knew was this: A real team, one bonded through purpose, can create something greater than any paycheck. Fewer than three percent of Division I athletes will ever play professionally. The majority of those who do will find themselves broke, divorced, or suffering from physical injuries or mental health problems within five years of retirement. Those who play for something larger, who build legacy, not just leverage, become more than professional athletes. They become ancestors of change.

Bobby continued to train through the storm of the country's reactions to his participation in the Sugar Bowl. While newspapers and politicians debated his existence, he kept his routine: film sessions, weight room, and practice until the light drained from the Pittsburgh sky. He knew that one mistake on the field could be weaponized, used as proof by those who preyed on his downfall. Dad's quiet leadership mirrored the civil rights ethos of the moment: defiance through dignity, power in restraint.

On the morning of December 27th, 1955, thirty-six players and five coaches boarded a Pan-American chartered plane at Greater Pittsburgh Airport (as it was called at the time). Their destination: New Orleans, the heart of the segregated South and the stage for the most historic game of their lives. Before embarking on this momentous journey, Bobby did not see himself as a headline or a symbol. He saw a son, a teammate, and a young man who learned from his family and community in Massillon that grace under pressure is the sharpest blade against hate.

The world he entered in New Orleans was a different planet. Separate hotels. Separate restaurants. Separate doors for entering the stadium. A city thick with tension, pride, and resistance to change. The January wind bit through New Orleans like it had a score to settle. The city glittered on the surface of the snow. Storefronts polished, the low winter sun catching brass railings and wrought-iron balconies. Bobby Grier stepped off the Pitt team bus and felt the city's hostility in his bones. His breath hung in the damp New Orleans air, but his core burned with a sharper awareness, one passed down through generations forced to read rooms for danger, not comfort. Below the Mason-Dixon Line, Black athletes were not just visitors. They were warnings.

Behind him, his white teammates laughed and wrestled over luggage, blissfully unaware of the coded stares from bystanders. They saw a football game ahead. Dad saw the architecture of segregation, hotel doors he could not walk through, restaurants that would only deny him entry, and stadium seats that only recently had been made available to Black people by history's slow hand. Word had spread. A Black player would take the field in the Sugar Bowl. The media was ablaze, the Sugar Bowl covering more front pages than Rosa Parks. Bobby's name traveled through homes, newsrooms, barber shops, and governors' mansions, growing louder with each retelling.

At the first practice in New Orleans, reporters clicked cameras, pens scribbled notes, and murmurs followed his every move. Bobby and the unified Pitt Panthers simply lined up, ran their routes, and hit their assignments, as if the entire country wasn't holding its breath. Bobby's cleats were not only leather and laces; they were a threat to the balance of power. One wrong snap of the ball could feel like a crack in the levees holding back centuries of oppression.

The University of Pittsburgh Panthers approached the 1956 Sugar Bowl with a mix of discipline and determination. It was their first bowl game invitation in nineteen years, a chance to reclaim a place among college football's elite. Coach Michelosen made sure that the Panthers treated the trip like a business mission, not a vacation. Upon landing in New Orleans around 1:15 p.m., the team went straight to Tulane University's practice facilities for their first workouts. Michelosen scheduled two-a-day practices in the lead-up to the game, morning and afternoon sessions designed to sharpen execution and keep his players focused under the weight of the national spotlight.

The Panthers carried quiet confidence into the week. They knew that Georgia Tech, a team seasoned in major bowl appearances, would be a formidable opponent. Oddsmakers favored the Yellow Jackets by a touchdown, but Michelosen remained steadfast. He told reporters that point spread "won't make any difference to us," a nod to the Panthers' mindset that steel town grit, discipline, and unity would define their performance, not predictions, yet Pitt remained underdogs.

The night before the Sugar Bowl, Bobby knelt beside his modest bed, separated from his team at Dillard University, thinking of the lessons his family had taught him. My dad had always played for his team and his community, and also for something larger than himself. Now, he was playing to unify an entire nation. After this game, he would come to realize that sports can change the world. Outside, the city of New Orleans hummed with revelry and tension. Inside, Bobby's prayer was simple: he prayed for strength more than safety. Bobby didn't come to run from the moment; he came to meet it. He asked for courage to carry the weight of history with grace, to represent his family, his team, and the countless faces in the stands and in the shadows, watching and hoping.

Come morning, the nation would not simply be watching a football game; they would be watching him. In that stillness of silence, before the roar, Dad understood that the line he was about to cross was bigger than any end zone. What Dad could not have known was that the Sugar Bowl itself would become larger than a football championship game. The Sugar Bowl would become a test of America itself. The roar of the crowd would be nothing compared to the echoes of the moment that was coming. At this point, in a sport long considered sacred and insulated, the lines of segregation were about to be tested under the glare of national attention.

REFLECTION QUESTIONS:

1. Have you ever witnessed or been part of a collective decision that defined societal expectations? What did it reveal about courage?
2. In what ways can institutions today learn from Pitt's decision to let players decide? What does it mean to stand behind someone fully, even when there are risks involved?

3. How does Bobby's quiet strength under intense social scrutiny provide lessons for modern athletes navigating the pressures of NIL fame, transfer portals, and social media spotlight?
4. How does Bobby's calm preparation the night before the Sugar Bowl embody leadership in moments of historic pressure? How can mental strength serve as a model for navigating personal and societal challenges today?
5. How can today's athletes embody the 1955–56 Pitt Panthers and advance progress (beyond the jersey, beyond the endorsement, beyond the now) as a team?

CHAPTER 5
ONE YARD FROM HISTORY

The air in New Orleans carried a strange electricity. On the surface, the city glittered with celebration. The Pitt and Georgia Tech bands tuned up in hotel lobbies, fans buzzed in anticipation, and the Sugar Bowl banners flapped in the breeze like a promise. Students draped in blue and gold or white and gold paraded Bourbon Street with youthful energy. And just beneath the jazz and confetti, hidden in plain sight, tension rolled like a gathering hurricane.

The stadium on game day was a mirror of a divided nation. Nearly 80,000 fans filled Tulane Stadium. In the Pitt section of the stadium, the crowd was integrated, and yet, this actually split the crowd even more. Some came to cheer. Some came to witness history with cautious pride. And some came with hate simmering in their eyes, determined that the old South would not give an inch. Bobby was not just playing in the Sugar Bowl; he was playing in the shadow of a dying, murderous, supremacist era, with a nation watching to see which would fall first: the segregationist groups or the illusion that sports were ever just a game.

And so, with the world watching, Dad laced up his cleats and stepped into history, not knowing if he would be tackled, cheered, or erased—only that the game was larger than football. The air itself felt electric and dangerous, as my father recalled. Bobby's cleats clicked on the concrete tunnel that smelled of sweat and dirt. There was an unspoken quiet, the calm before the storm. This was no ordinary game.

The Pitt and Tech bands spelled out "NCAA 50" not only as a tribute to the association's fiftieth anniversary, but also in a show of unity during a divided and tumultuous time. The Panthers ran out first, blue and gold flashing against the harsh winter light. As Bobby jogged out under the Southern sky, the stadium roar sounded like a clash of two Americas, one desperate to hold the line, the other straining to break free. The Sugar Bowl was supposed to be a game. Instead, it became a mirror, and in that mirror, America saw its reflection, flawed and divided, but shifting.

Pitt and Georgia Tech bands spelling "NCAA 50" at the 1956 Sugar Bowl

While the nation tuned in for kickoff, the real game, the one that could rewrite the rules of America, had already begun. This was just the beginning. As Bobby took his first step onto that field, the weight of history pressed against his chest, and the question lingered in the frosty January air: Was America ready to follow him across this line?

The game began as a defensive slugfest, with Bobby making the first tackle on the initial kick off. Mud clung to cleats. Every yard felt earned with blood and grit. Early in the first quarter, Bobby met a Georgia Tech fullback head-on, halting him for no gain. Midway through the first quarter, he slipped through a hole on offense, dragging two defenders for a first down, the crowd roaring in mixed voices. Every snap was a brushstroke against a segregated canvas. The game remained scoreless. A storm brewed inside Bobby, not of anger, but of determination. He understood what was at stake. He was not only running plays; he was running a race that someone else had started, and the world was watching.

Then came the moment that history remembers.

Bobby Grier breaking barriers in the 1956 Sugar Bowl

"*I was outside in what we called an 'Eagle' defense,*" said Bobby Grier. "*I went back with the player, and when I turned to look up and see where the ball was, I got pushed in the back. The ball was over his head, and I was lying on the ground, then he (referee Frank Lowry—no relation) threw a flag and said I pushed him ... with me lying on the ground, looking up and the ball over both our heads.*"

Don Ellis (Georgia Tech fullback) said, "*I got behind him. Then, when I turned around to look for the pass, he shoved me in the stomach, knocking me off stride. It was a fine pass, and I think I could have caught it.*"

The controversial pass interference, Don Ellis (number 89) and Bobby Grier (foreground), 1956 Sugar Bowl

At the time, the film was inconclusive, but it indicated Grier may have been out of position, stumbled, and fallen a few yards in front of Ellis. The official call was pass interference. A roar of protest erupted from the stands as the ball was placed on the 1-yard line. Immediately, the reporter sitting next to legendary New Orleans sports writer Buddy Diliberto began typing a bulletin that read, "Bobby Grier, the first Negro to play in the Sugar Bowl, was roundly booed by a crowd of 80,000 spectators today in Tulane Stadium." Diliberto caught a glance at the reporter's writing. "You don't REALLY believe that, do you?" he shouted, incredulously. "They're booing the call, not Grier!"

After Pitt was penalized a half-yard for being offsides, Wade Mitchell, quarterback, defensive back, and kicker for Tech, followed the surge of his line and made it into the endzone by inches. He then added the extra point. Bobby was the leading rusher, finishing with fifty-one rushing yards.

And, just like that, the game was over. A flag. A yard. A legacy.

Check out this QR Code to watch play-by-play highlights of the 1956 Sugar Bowl and the controversial play that cemented Bobby Grier in the history books.

Bobby did not weep for himself. He wept for his team, for the burden he could not shed, for the invisible battle he could not block or outrun. Photographers captured his quiet grace as reporters crowded in. He raised his open hands to show how he had been pushed in the back. He was calm and measured. No excuses. No bitterness. Just dignity. Then something remarkable happened. Georgia Tech players, who had stood firm against their own governor to let Bobby play, shook his hand and invited him to sit with them at the postgame banquet. Coach Bobby Dodd praised his courage and grace, and in that moment, in the most segregated city in America, respect broke down barriers before the law had even addressed equality.

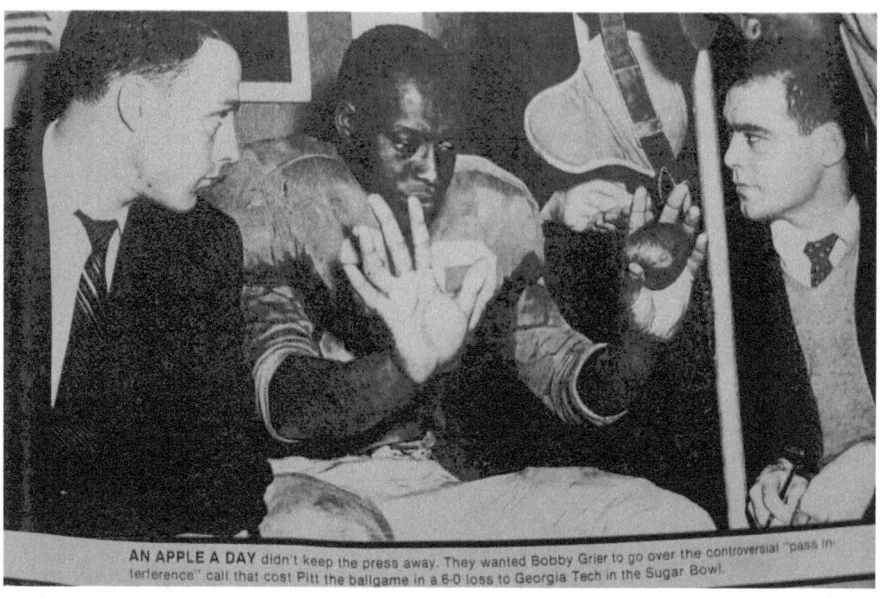

AN APPLE A DAY didn't keep the press away. They wanted Bobby Grier to go over the controversial "pass interference" call that cost Pitt the ballgame in a 6-0 loss to Georgia Tech in the Sugar Bowl.

Bobby Grier, post-game interview, 1956 Sugar Bowl

The banquet room was filled with clinking glasses, soft jazz drifting from a corner, and the hum of conversation that carried both pride and intensity. Bobby, in his Pitt blazer, carried himself with the same humility and dignity that he had shown all season. He shook hands, posed for photographs, and listened as white players and coaches, many of whom had never shared such social space with a Black man, spoke words of admiration that would have been unthinkable just a few years earlier. Every waitstaff member in the room, being Black, shared a longing glance with Bobby, grateful for his stance and the hope that they could one day be in a position like his.

After dinner, the evening transitioned to a postgame dance, the kind of celebration that typically blurred the lines between victory and relief. In the 1950s South, boisterous parties like this were for white men and women to let loose and have fun. A Black man seen socializing or even standing too close to white women invited danger that could come with fatal consequences. How, after all, could the white men enjoy their victory when forced to suffer through the unthinkable encounter of a Black man exchanging polite conversation with white women? Though the team had invited him, for Dad, this was a line he could not cross. His coaches and community allies quietly urged him not to stay for the dance. Instead, Dad left immediately after the Bowl dinner for a special affair at Dillard University's campus. Dixie sports writers went to extremes in praising Dad's decision not to attend the Sugar Bowl dance thrown for Pitt and Georgia Tech players in New Orleans at the St. Charles Hotel. My father understood the unspoken rules of survival. Some doors opened for a handshake, but not yet for entry.

President Albert W. Dent personally met him again after the banquet. That night, the Black community of New Orleans gave my father a hero's welcome. His fraternity brothers of Kappa Alpha Psi at Dillard, decked out in crimson and cream, hosted a private party in his honor. Dad and his "nupe" (a common nickname for members) frat brothers were stepping, spinning their canes overhead. Jazz drifted from phonographs, and the rooms pulsed with pride. In those spaces, Dad could exhale. He could laugh. He could dance. He could feel the full weight of what his presence on that field meant to people who had been waiting their whole lives for a moment like this.

The city that tried to divide him could not touch his joy. In those rooms, among his own, Dad was not a controversy or a headline. He was a champion and a living piece of history.

The Sugar Bowl was not supposed to be historic. However, history does not ask for permission. What began as a game would become a reckoning. Before the players even took to the field, the backlash in the South came fast and furious. In retaliation, Georgia and Louisiana quickly and quietly drafted laws banning future integrated games. By July of 1956, both states had drafted laws that they would only play southern teams in the Sugar Bowl. A pyrrhic victory that proved just how seismic Bobby's quiet courage had become. Other laws passed in their wake would push back integration in college sports for years to come. These decisions were influenced by Louisiana Governor Huey P. Long, who was in office in the 1930s. He enacted laws designed to suppress Black voters, requiring constitutional interpretations meant to intimidate and disenfranchise. His brother, Earl Long, serving as Governor of Louisiana in 1956, continued Huey's onslaught of hatred. Of course, these very laws eventually backfired, ensnaring white voters as well.

In both sport and politics, attempts to hold one group back often end up damaging the fabric of society for everyone. The college football segregation laws were revoked in 1959, and the sport eventually integrated, over time, throughout the 1960s and early 1970s. The next integrated Sugar Bowl game took place in 1965, with LSU playing Syracuse, which had two Black players on its team. Still, the echoes of this pattern can be felt in modern America, where policies or barriers aimed at exclusion—whether in voting, education, sports, or economic opportunity—often erode trust and limit progress for a larger population, proving that a nation divided against itself ultimately weakens its own foundation.

Despite these attempts to silence him, Bobby never lashed out. He did not need to. His very presence was a challenge to the status quo. As Dad stepped onto that field, under the Southern sky thick with Southern racial pride and tension, the question was not just who would win, but whether America was ready to change or not. Bobby walked out of that stadium without a trophy, but he left a giant. His presence on that field had cut a path through history, showing the power of silent courage. One penalty may have changed the scoreboard, but Bobby Grier changed the game of football forever, planting seeds for future generations of athletes who now play under the bright lights with NIL deals, media campaigns, and platforms to speak out against injustices.

Modern players monetize their name and image. Bobby Grier risked his name, his safety, his life, and his future for a simple right: to play football. And yet, on that humid New Orleans night, a truth emerged as clear as a stadium whistle: One yard could change a game, but courage could change a country. Still, Bobby's next steps would echo far beyond the Sugar Bowl, rippling into the very heart of American sports and civil rights history.

REFLECTION QUESTIONS:

1. How does Bobby's experience of risking everything for the right to play reflect the challenges of today's athletes, despite NIL deals and modern visibility?
2. In what ways can silent courage and performance create more lasting change than public statements or protests?
3. How did Bobby's calm response to the controversial penalty call demonstrate his approach to challenging racism through dignity rather than confrontation?
4. What does Bobby's Sugar Bowl experience reveal about sports' power to expose societal injustice and force national conversations about change?

CHAPTER 6
LEGACY IN MOTION

In the locker room beneath Tulane Stadium, steam curled from the showers and silence lingered like smoke. Twenty-three-year-old Bobby sat in his gear, silently, with tears in his eyes, the sound of his heartbeat louder than the roar of the Sugar Bowl crowd. In that quiet, unassuming moment, Dad realized that the field had changed, but the fight had only just begun. He stood in the center of it all, not by choice, but by destiny. He did not gloat; he did not smile. He simply sat still, savoring the moment. Around him, teammates moved like shadows, some pacing, others staring into the concrete. No one quite knew what to say. The game was over, but the war had just begun.

News cameras outside the stadium clicked like machine guns as Bobby left for Dillard University. Sportswriters sharpened their pens. In the swirl of southern heat and national scrutiny, Bobby had become more than a football player. He was a living headline, a symbol both revered and reviled. The moment

America latched onto was not his historic entrance, but that one call. The flag. The pass interference. It was not only a penalty; it was a flashpoint.

In Pittsburgh, Birmingham, Detroit, Chicago, Baltimore, Los Angeles, and Harlem, Black families huddled around radios and television, shaking their heads. Was it fair? Was it fear? Was it justice or just a desperate attempt to hold onto the old playbook of white superiority? Some still argue the call was unfair, a product of the moment and the pressure. Some say it was simply a bad call in a bad game. Yet, for many watching, especially in the segregated corners of the stadium, it was a reminder that even the rules could bend underneath the weight of prejudice.

The real noise, the one that would not die, was Bobby's enduring presence in places it had never been before. It shook pews in Southern churches, rattled headlines in the North, and sent shockwaves through the quiet halls of state capitols. In locker rooms from Louisiana to Los Angeles, young Black athletes whispered Bobby's name not only in celebration, but in recognition. He had played not just for victory, but for visibility. Now, coaches, teammates, and opponents alike had to reckon with it.

In the days following the Sugar Bowl, letters to Bobby poured in by the dozens. Some were scrawled in trembling cursive, spewing hate like a toxin. Others were written on fine stationery, their praise wrapped in genteel surprise: *"Never thought I would say this, but you played with class, son."* There were telegrams from soldiers, postcards from grandmothers, and one handwritten note from a ten-year-old in Ohio: *"Dear Mr. Grier, thank you for being brave. My dad said you made history. I think you made it better."*

One letter, shown below, traveled an extensive 2,500 miles from Springfield, Oregon, to the University of Pittsburgh, full of support for Bobby:

"Dear Mr. Grier:

This is just a note to tell you how distressed we were over the recent controversy that arose prior to the Pitt Tech game. In our ignorance we had supposed no man could rise to the position of Governor who so flagrantly defied both the Constitution and the Bible. Now we have just finished reading the write-up of the game and that heartbreaking call. You have every reason to be bitter and discouraged but we hope you won't be and the fact that we and all our friends (even tho' we are strangers) are on your side will ease your unhappiness a little bit.

Yours very sincerely,
Mr. & Mrs. Roy DeWitt"

Letter from Mr. and Mrs. DeWitt, January 3, 1956, Springfield, Oregon

Not all the responses were positive. Dad read every letter, even the cruel ones. Especially the cruel ones. He knew that behind each slur was proof that he had pierced something deeper than football. He had unsettled an entire belief system with nothing more than a helmet, shoulder pads, and unwavering composure.

Within twenty-four hours of the game, Governor Griffin delivered another furious address. Though masked in political language, the sentiment was plain: the presence of a Negro athlete on a Southern football field was not to be repeated. Yet, the newspapers had already spoken louder than any dog whistle of eugenics. History did not wait for permission. Neither did the press. Newspapers flooded the streets the next morning, some cautious, some caustic. One powerful headline cut through them all like a steel blade:

"News for Georgia Governor: Negro Athlete Here to Stay."

It was not just a headline. It was a verdict, a declaration, a prophecy.

What the article exposed, brilliantly and brutally, was a fear that could not be disguised by Southern charm or political spin, that integration was not just coming, it was already here. In stadiums, in schools, and in the hearts of fans who no longer saw Black athletes as anomalies, but as champions. In plain, unsparing terms, the article made one thing clear: The days of pretending Black athletes did not belong on America's biggest stages were over. No amount of deflections could change the fact that the tide had turned. The ball was not just in play on the gridiron; it was rolling through the very soul of America.

The photo beneath the headline showed Bobby mid-stride, helmet in hand, walking along through a tunnel as flashes burst around him. His eyes were steady. His posture was calm. But beneath the surface, America was unraveling. The Sugar Bowl was no longer just a game. It had become a cultural earthquake. Fault lines stretched from New Orleans to the White House. On college campuses, debates ignited. At dining tables, tensions rose. And in Southern statehouses, phone lines buzzed with urgency. Segregationists whispered of betrayal. Activists spoke of revolution.

The Sugar Bowl headlines had rippled beyond sports pages. National editorial boards debated the call. University presidents squirmed. White Southern senators fumed. Perhaps the most important article of all was published after a private screening of the game films, which effectively showed that there was no pass interference. The call was, indeed, bad. Of course, the article was too little, too late.

> "Observers at a private screening of the game films saw the disputed play section of the film 25 times in both slow motion and natural speed. It showed that Grier did not make bodily contact with Ellis in the end zone, the place it would have had to occur given the type of penalty called. The pictures showed Ellis managed to get behind Grier and had a clear shot at the ball had it been thrown accurately by Mitchell, who was passing from the Pitt 33. The film showed Grier stumbled and fell two yards in front of Ellis."

Article in *The Pittsburgh Press*, February 5, 1956

With the game over, life went on. Life on Pitt's campus shifted subtly, then suddenly. To the average student, it was business as usual—midterms, cafeteria chatter, spring semester schedules. But for Bobby, things did not return to normal; they evolved into something else. Professors and administrators nodded in passing. White students, once indifferent, lingered to talk after class. People stared longer now—some with admiration, others with confusion. Some asked for his autograph. Others carried themselves with the kind of silent resentment that never made it to words, but could be felt in a room like static electricity. The cafeteria line became a litmus test for change. Some moved forward with him, while others stepped aside. He could not blend in anymore, even if he wanted to.

Meanwhile, far from campus, a different kind of currency began to circulate: Dad's image. Quietly at first, a sports feature in *Jet* magazine, a mention in *TIME* magazine, and editorial debates in the *Pittsburgh Post-Gazette* and *The New York Times*. He was more than just a photo in a newspaper; he stood for something bigger. He was a real person who had gone through this experience and came out stronger on the other side. He was a metaphor for what was possible and what still needed to be fought for. He did not ask for it, but the world had decided: Bobby Grier now belonged to history, and to the future.

Amidst the friction, new forces were awakening. Church groups held prayer vigils, not for protection, but for progress. Black educators wrote op-eds calling Bobby *"the unexpected curriculum."* A coalition of clergy from Pittsburgh to Atlanta whispered, "This changes everything." The world around Bobby pulsed with a new awareness. Every glance carried weight. Every handshake was a statement. He was no longer just Bobby the fullback. He became the torchbearer of what was coming next because sometimes the loudest plays come after the game has ended.

Pitt's administration continually received letters for years, even following Dad's graduation from the university. Some of them were venomous. Others were tear-stained and grateful. A note came in from a mother in Topeka: *"My boy taped your picture to his locker. He says he wants to be brave like you."* Another, from a veteran in Alabama: *"I fought beside colored boys in WWII. What you did took the same kind of courage."* A group of educators from Atlanta wrote to Pitt's administration: *"What Mr. Grier has done on the field, we are teaching in our schools."* A pastor from Harlem invoked his name in a sermon. Even a coach from Texas quietly asked, "Can our boys talk to him?"

But perhaps the most unexpected letter came from a dean at a historically Black college in Mississippi: *"Your steps on the gridiron echoed into classrooms across the South. We are using your story in our lectures. You are not just playing football. You are playing for history."*

It was the first time Bobby saw a path beyond the field, not just for himself, but for those watching. The game had ended, but a new arena was opening. Not stadiums, but institutions. Not touchdowns, but transformation. Coaches began talking, quietly, about recruiting more Black athletes. Sportswriters looked back at the Sugar Bowl and began calling it "the integration game." Corporations noticed too. Not because they cared about civil rights, but because they cared about the public eye. Some wanted Bobby for "speaking engagements." He was even offered a magazine cover. Bobby declined the gloss and chose grit.

He spoke instead to student groups, church circles, and quiet rooms filled with athletes who had never seen someone who looked like them get a shot that big. Throughout most of his adult life, my father continued to choose to help others. Assisting non-profits to help struggling families receive food, volunteering with youth sport camps and teams, and ultimately becoming a caregiver to his wife of 59 years Dorothy, later in life. Throughout his journey, he continued to carry the same humility and drive for community and equality.

One evening, in a candle-lit church basement in Homewood, a teenage boy raised his hand after Bobby finished speaking.

"Mister Grier, do you think it will matter?" he said.

Dad paused. He saw his younger self in the boy's eyes—wide, hopeful, and weary.

"If it did not already matter," Bobby said, "you would not be here asking that question."

The room fell silent, but something passed between them, a current, invisible but undeniable. The next day, that boy skipped school and walked six miles to ask the coach how to try out for the football team.

The ripples had begun.

Bobby stayed grounded. He still went to class. Still trained. Inside, however, he knew something had taken root. His courage, once required just to walk into a stadium, was now a seed being planted in thousands of lives. He gave young men, and the people watching them, a new possibility to imagine. Somewhere on the edge of the field, just out of view, a new generation was warming up. Wearing cleats, carrying dreams, and looking for someone to show them how to break the line without breaking themselves.

Across the country, a new kind of strategy session was underway. College boards, ad execs, student unions, even civil rights leaders, started asking not "What happened?" at the Sugar Bowl, but rather "What comes next?" They did not know it yet, but Bobby's quiet bravery was building a blueprint. One day, it would become known as NIL, more focused on branding than anything else. Bobby carried something bigger: NIL, where the "L" stands for Legacy. For Bobby, it was simply a choice. Stand for something, or watch it fall apart. My father had no agent, no brand deals, no camera crew. His name, image, and likeness were worth more than endorsement; they represented endurance. And that kind of legacy does not expire. It passes on.

REFLECTION QUESTIONS:

1. What does the headline "Negro Athlete Here to Stay" symbolize in the broader context of the civil rights era, and why was this declaration so powerful in 1956?
2. What does it mean to transform from athlete to cultural icon? Do you see Bobby's journey as an honor or a burden? How does this relate to building a lasting legacy versus seeking momentary fame?
3. How do moments in sports sometimes become turning points for broader political and cultural

change? What parallels do you see with modern athlete-activists, such as Colin Kaepernick?

4. How does Bobby's story unite people across geography, race, and profession? What does this reveal about the power of individual courage to rise above perceived limitations?

5. What emotions did Bobby's post-game experiences evoke for you? How do the cultural tensions he faced (both internally and externally) mirror today's struggles with visibility, justice, and representation?

6. What modern-day equivalents exist today where athletes (or any public figure) must choose between seeking the spotlight and staying authentic to their values and heart? Do you find this in your own life?

CHAPTER 7
THE NEXT FIELD

Somewhere between the constant pressure to perform on the field and heading to the U.S. Air Force, Bobby's next chapter began with love. In the quieter months at Pitt, Bobby found himself connecting with someone who didn't much care to talk about touchdowns or headlines. Dorothy "Dot" was part of the Delta Sigma Theta Sorority, and Bobby was part of the newly formed Kappa Alpha Psi Fraternity. They met at a mixer that Bobby almost skipped.

Dot studied education and later went on to earn her PhD at the University of Pittsburgh in the same field of study. She was a sharp, spirited young woman who moved through campus with a quiet, soft conviction. She loved music and was full of curiosity. She did not treat Bobby like a symbol; she asked him what books he liked. She asked him about what scared him. She listened like she was building a future out of every answer—because she was.

Over time, they moved from shared study sessions to long walks up Cardiac Hill. The courtship was simple. Notes tucked in books. Walks near the Cathedral of Learning. Exploring the Cathedral's International rooms. Slowly sipping coffee at diners where, even if they were allowed inside, they were treated poorly. Facing the harshness of the world together only drew Bobby and Dot closer. In a chaotic world full of lynchings and murders of young black men, Bobby found sanctuary in Dot. Her laugh softened the sharp edges of the world around him. In her presence, Bobby was just Bobby, not history, not defiance, not "the Negro athlete."

My dad once told me, "She knew me from playing football, and I would always see her with her head buried in a book. She thought I was a dumb jock, but was proud of me playing on the national stage, representing Pitt."

In 1957, they married in a modest ceremony away from the cameras and campus halls. Pitt basketball star Julius Pegues served as best man, and Julius's then girlfriend and soon-to-be wife, Dr. Wennette Pegues, served as maid of honor. Bobby and Dot built a legacy louder than any headline that endured for decades. Dot would later travel to games with Bobby as he was honored by Pitt. Together, they had two children and one amazing grandchild (my daughter). What began as a cautious conversation grew into love that defied the times. Nearly sixty years of life, love, and legacy would follow.

Shortly after graduating from the University of Pittsburgh and marrying Dot, Bobby joined the Air Force. For Bobby, it was more than a career path; it was a chance to serve his country in a uniform that promised equality. It looked like a door to the future. But history has a way of leaving fingerprints on the present.

Only a few years earlier, Black veterans returning from war were the most targeted men in America. They had fought tyranny overseas, only to be hunted at home, dragged from buses, beaten in uniform, lynched for the audacity of wearing the nation's colors. In the Jim Crow South, a Black man in uniform was not a symbol of honor; to many, he was a threat.

54th Fighter Group, U.S. Air Force

Bobby knew these stories. They were not whispered folktales; they were warnings passed down from generation to generation at dinner tables, in barber chairs, and at church. Joining the military was not just service to the country; it was stepping into a different type of spotlight, one that could draw pride or danger, sometimes both on the same day.

The Air Force was integrated on paper thanks to President Truman's 1948 order, but on the field, there was still a divide. Certain bases felt like home; others felt like away games that were dangerous and unwelcoming. Outside the gates, the same old Jim Crow rules applied. Even the mess hall could be friendly in the morning and hostile by the evening.

Bobby Grier's official U.S. Air Force photo

Still, football found Bobby. Military bases had their own teams: fierce, talented squads that played for bragging rights across commands. Generals acted like NFL owners, trading players between bases, the way pro teams shuffle rosters. Some generals guarded their star players like prized draft picks; others lured talent from rival bases, with the quiet pull of influence. Bobby was stationed at several domestic and international bases, including Seymour Johnson AFB (North Carolina), Loring AFB (Maine, now closed), Luke AFB (Arizona), Ellington AFB (Texas), Ramstein AFB (Germany), Osan AB (South Korea), and Kadena AB (Japan). Talent was currency, and a good running back could find himself "transferred" in the name of military readiness. Really, it was for the sake of the scoreboard.

The name "Bobby Grier" still carried weight. The legend of the Sugar Bowl still followed him, and on the field, rank did not matter; touchdowns did. These games were far from friendly competition. They were showcases, morale boosters, and subtle power plays between officers.

Bobby Grier at military base football practice

For Bobby, suiting up again was both a gift and a test. It let him keep the game alive, where the hits carried more weight. He had to keep proving himself as the field was not so level, yet the rules were clear. But it also reminded Bobby that what you did on the field lived alongside politics. A transfer could come with opportunity or isolation, depending on which colors you wore that week.

Off the field, the quiet and not-so-quiet battles continued. The Equal Justice Initiative's own records show that from WWI through Korea, hundreds of Black veterans were murdered just for wearing the uniform. That risk did not disappear in 1957 and, in many cases, got worse. Wearing the Air Force Blues could open doors on one side of town and invite murderous mobs on another.

Bobby Grier Receiving the U.S. Air Force Commendation

Bobby's years at Pitt and in the Air Force sharpened him. They taught him to read people the way offenses read defenses to know where the pressure was coming from before the snap of the ball. He learned that leadership was less about the rank you wore and more about the trust you inspired. And just as in football, some teammates would block for you, while others would miss the block and call it bad luck.

Beyond the bases, America and the world were changing. The Montgomery Bus Boycott (1955–56) proved economic boycotts were effective, and the Little Rock Nine (1957) just wanted to go to school. Bobby's courage paid out in something more profound: a legacy and the respect of those who knew what it took to wear both the helmet and uniform with pride.

The Air Force was not the loudest chapter in his life, but it may have been the most complex. Twelve Black men in his group, including Bobby, wanted to be pilots. The sergeant told them that eleven of them would "wash out," or in other words, wouldn't make it. The game wasn't over. He was reminded that whether on the gridiron or in the barracks, proving yourself is about more than the score. Bobby spent most of his time in the military working on radars and missiles. He entered the Air Force as an officer and retired in 1968 as a captain.

After the Air Force, Bobby worked as a blast-furnace supervisor at U.S. Steel, but he stayed involved with the Pitt Panthers. He regularly attended the games and could often be found on the field or in the locker room, sharing words of wisdom with the players. As a result, he did some recruiting for the football team. It was the early 1970s, and though Bobby was no longer wearing football cleats, he was still carrying the weight of social progress. In this role, the University knew something unspoken: If Bobby Grier vouched for a young man, he was not just betting on talent; he was investing in a legacy.

The first time Bobby saw Tony Dorsett play for Hopewell High School in Aliquippa, Pennsylvania, Bobby was in awe. Tony was not running; he was gliding, where everyone else seemed in slow motion. Tony slipped through defenders like water through fingers. He moved like poetry with a helmet and pads on, touchdown after touchdown. He was unstoppable.

Tony was not just any recruit. He was *the* recruit. Tony stood at five feet, eleven inches tall and 192 pounds. He was a phenom with feet like fire and a determination made from steel. Every school wanted him, but Pitt needed him. And Bobby knew it.

The meeting was quiet at Tony's house with his parents, Wes and Myrtle. Tony didn't speak much, and neither did Bobby. There was a stillness between them, an understanding that needed no translation.

"This school," Bobby finally said, "did not always look like it does now. I bled on this field before it welcomed men like us. But I believed it would."

Tony looked up.

Bobby continued, "I'm not asking you to be me. I'm asking you to be *better*. And I believe you will be."

That was all. No dramatic pitch. No promises, just truth.

Tony Dorsett committed to Pitt. The rest is written in bronze: Tony led the Panthers to the national championship in 1976 and became Pitt's first Heisman Trophy winner. Twelve seasons in the NFL and inductions into both the Pro Football and College Football Hall of Fame. Every record he broke carried a thread woven by Bobby's quiet hand.

Bobby Grier and Tony Dorsett at the University of Pittsburgh's Century of Change Gala, 2011

Years later, when asked about his decision, Tony said, "*I came here because of what Bobby Grier stood for. He didn't push me. He showed me.*"

In many ways, Bobby never stopped recruiting—not only athletes, but also for his belief in others. He recruited young men into manhood. He recruited communities into courage. He invested in his recruits and led them to greatness. Through every whispered hallway and campus corridor, his presence lingered, not loud, but *undeniable*. Real legacy does not shout; it echoes. Some men leave their mark through their actions. Bobby did that and then some.

REFLECTION QUESTIONS:

1. How did military football culture mirror the politics and power plays of professional sports?
2. What risks did Black veterans face simply by wearing the uniform—risks that today's athletes might take for granted?
3. In what ways can sports act as a bridge in divided institutions like the military?
4. How might Bobby's dual identity as a serviceman and athlete have shaped his resilience?
5. Who are the people watching your example (your "recruits"), and how might you mentor them with purpose?
6. How does one generation's courage seed another's breakthrough?
7. How can true influence be passed intentionally without being loud or self-promoting?

CHAPTER 8
THE TORCH AND THE TUNNEL

The past does not fade. It resonates. From a freshman locker room in 1953 to a roaring stadium at the 1956 Sugar Bowl, Bobby's footsteps did not echo alone. They struck chords that would later stir greatness in others. Quiet, unshakeable, steady. Dad's walk through fire laid a trail many would one day sprint.

Johnny Majors, a Tennessee native and Heisman runner-up, carried his own burden of legacy when he arrived at Pitt. He served as head coach from 1973 to 1976 and again from 1993 to 1996. Though he never really spoke about Bobby publicly, he often told players in private that there was one name he wished the nation talked about more. "Bobby didn't just change football," he would say with his Tennessee drawl. "He changed what we thought a man could be under pressure." Behind closed doors, Majors credited Bobby's restraint, grace, and mental toughness as foundational to the new Pitt culture he was trying to instill.

Johnny Majors and Bobby Grier at Heinz Field

Then came Rickey Jackson, raw and relentless. He was a linebacker for Pittsburgh from 1977 to 1980 and had fists like anvils and instincts like radar. Rickey was known to snarl before tackles. In interviews, he'd nod when Bobby's name came up. "I was unaware, but amazed by Bobby's story. All new recruits need to know his story," he once said. Rickey didn't just play through pain. He played through history, and he knew it.

Then, there's Dan Marino, who played quarterback at Pittsburgh from 1979 to 1982. The cannon-armed Pittsburgh legend often visited campus with a swagger born from the city's steel and soot. Even Dan, never one to idolize easily, would later share that he admired Bobby's ability to perform under heat hotter than any NFL stadium lights. *"When I think pressure,"* Marino told a local paper, *"I think Grier in New Orleans."*

NO GRIER, NO GAME

Bobby Grier and Dan Marino

Bobby's legacy lived on.

In 2002, a young wide receiver—quick, ambitious, and inked with symbols of both faith and rebellion—transferred to Pitt. His name was Larry Fitzgerald, and he walked into a program laced with shadows of titans. Larry played at Pitt for one season before entering the NFL. Before every practice, in the tunnel of the Pitt stadium, a mural of a large, domineering Bobby Grier stared back at him. In the silence before the snap and in the weight of expectation, he felt Bobby's legacy. In truth, progress and pressure often show up with a fist bump or a hug. Larry had the ball tucked under his arm, his back straight, and his gaze locked ahead. Not a warrior by choice, a warrior by necessity. Larry had not yet met my father in person, but when he first learned about him, everything clicked. "You mean the guy who broke the color barrier in a bowl game *here*?" he asked. "That's the kind of heritage they never teach in orientation, but should."

My father attended as many Pitt games as he could. Watching young Black men, like Larry, was like seeing himself on the field. When Larry and his Panthers teammates took the field, the crowd stood in applause, not just for the beloved Panthers, but for the memory sewn into the seams of branded jerseys. Somewhere in the echo between cheers and stadium lights, a truth pulsed loud and clear: Legacy does not fade. It multiplies. Dot and Bobby sat in the front row; her hands clasped over a well-worn Pitt scarf, Bobby wearing his signature Pitt tie. She smiled. She had seen this moment coming.

In 2011, Bobby and Larry met in person, back at the school where they both played. The lights of Heinz Field shimmered like a memory for Bobby. It had been decades since he stood under these stadium lights, but his shadow still had not faded. If anything, it had grown longer, stretching into classrooms, locker rooms, and lives that had not yet been born when he made history. Bobby and Larry were back at their old stomping grounds to attend a party honoring and celebrating one hundred years of Black athletes at Pitt: the Century of Change Gala. More than two hundred former athletes attended the event held in their honor, including Bobby and Larry, among many other notable athletes, including:

- Herb Douglas: Pitt's oldest living African-American athlete (eighty-nine years old in 2011 when he was honored at the Century of Change Gala; he passed away in 2023); first African-American Football walk-on and Olympic Bronze Medalist in the 1948 London Summer Games; inducted into the Pitt Hall of Fame.
- Reverend Jimmy Joe Robinson: Pitt's First African-American football recruit; to this date, he holds Pitt's punt return record with a ninety-yard punt return against Penn State in 1945.
- Sam Clancy: Only player in Pitt basketball history to compile 1,000 points and 1,000 rebounds in a career; Gold Medalist in the 1979 Pan American Games; successfully altered his professional career path and went on to play eleven seasons in the NFL; inducted into the Pitt Hall of Fame.
- Hugh Green: Three-time All-American; winner of the Maxwell Award; the only Division I defensive lineman to be runner-up for the Heisman Trophy; all-time sacks leader at Pitt, and ranks second all-time in tackles; inducted into the Pitt Hall of Fame.
- Julius Pegues: First African-American men's basketball player at Pitt.
- Trecia-Kaye Smith: Inducted into the Pitt Hall of Fame; fifteen-time All-American track performer; NCAA Division I Most Outstanding Student-Athlete; came to the gala from London.

This night was not just about the past; it was about the handoff. A reminder of legacy and a promise for what the future holds for Black athletes.

Bobby Grier and Larry Fitzgerald at the University of Pittsburgh's Century of Change Gala, 2011

Across generations, across positions, across divides, Bobby's story became the soft thump behind every cleat digging into Pitt's turf. Not all of them knew his name when they arrived. But everyone knew who he was by the time they left. The statue has not yet been raised, but in the weight rooms, in the locker stalls, and in the murmured mentor moments, it was already standing.

To complete the picture of Bobby's impact, we must return to those who built it alongside him. The locker rooms filled with steam, leather, and anticipation had long since given way to dust-kissed trophies lining the living room shelves and cleats stored away in a closet. In the hearts of those who bled Panther Blue beside Bobby, memories live just beneath the surface, like a playbook etched into the soul. The team would often reconnect at Heinz Field. They were honored regularly—typically on milestone anniversaries of the 1956 Sugar Bowl game—and would join each other on the field and reminisce about the game.

1956 Sugar Bowl Team being honored at Heinz Field

Bob Rosborough, one of Bobby's linemen at Pitt and a longtime friend, quietly reflected decades later on plays that could have won them the 1956 Sugar Bowl. "Bobby didn't say much; he never needed to. He walked into that huddle like he belonged, even when half the world said he didn't," Bob remembered.

Gordy Oliver, another one of Bobby's teammates, reflected

with amusement on the risque picture (shown below), published in the *Pittsburgh Post-Gazette* days before the Sugar Bowl, of the team sitting on the training tables getting their ankles taped before practice in their jock straps. He remembered the roar of 80,000 screaming fans at the nationally televised game. Gordy shared, "There were no banners. No coaches saying, Thank you. But I remember the day he walked into the weight room after that Sugar Bowl, standing tall and proud, yet determined not to let the Sugar Bowl be the last chapter in his life. Still asking how the younger players were doing."

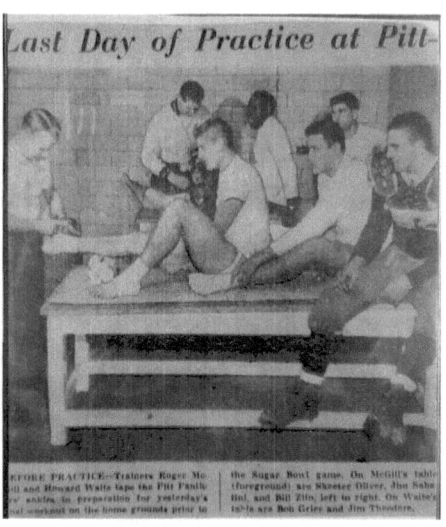

Pittsburgh Panthers before the 1956 Sugar Bowl, *Pittsburgh Post-Gazette*

In his first season as the Panthers' head coach, John Michelosen said the following, which we retrieved from an archived letter, as he has long since passed away: *"He was our constant. The press did not know what to do with him. But we did. A strong kid from an Ohio powerhouse school. He played smart, and above all else, he played as a team."*

Decades later, Bobby's story reads like a masterclass in how to move forward in fractured times. My father did not just play football; he modeled how to lead through storms, both political and societal. He proved that legacy is not earned through applause, but through alignment between values and action, humility and courage. That matters now more than ever.

Bobby is part of the Sugar Bowl Hall of Fame, the Pitt Athletics Hall of Fame, and the Western Pennsylvania Sports Hall of Fame. He appeared in countless TV interviews and was part of ESPN's award-winning documentary, *College Football 150*. Bobby went on to work with the prestigious Elizabeth Dole Foundation, which provides support to military and veteran caregivers. He was featured in another award-winning documentary, *Sky Blossom: Diaries of the Next Greatest Generation*, which highlighted young caregivers of disabled veterans. Bobby was an advocate not only for veterans and their health, but also for over five million caregivers of veterans in America. His legacy lives on—in his accomplishments, yes, but more importantly, in all the lives he has touched, both those who know him and those who know of him.

In an era when America boiled over with fear, hate, and division, Bobby walked into history, not with anger, but with grace. Not as a symbol, but as a son, a student, and a teammate. Simply by staying in the game, he rewrote it. Bobby never needed to raise his voice. He was the message.

Today's world is more disconnected and digitally distracted than Bobby's ever was. Yet somehow, the silence of his strength still speaks louder than trending hashtags or viral outrage. His walk through the tunnel that cold day in 1956 was not just for Pitt. It was a silent blueprint for every young athlete wondering if their platform matters. A new generation now wears the jersey, following in Bobby's footsteps.

Bobby's legacy reminds us that NIL is about more than Name, Image, and Likeness. It's about **Narrative, Integrity, and Legacy**.

In a divided world, my father's legacy isn't a moment to admire; it is a manual to follow.

REFLECTION QUESTIONS:

1. What does Bobby's influence across generations reveal about the long arc of social impact? How does Bobby's impact on Marino, Fitzgerald, and others show that greatness isn't always passed down in stats, but in stories?
2. Why do you think it is often the quiet trailblazers who lay the loudest foundations? What might that say about our need to honor the unseen or overlooked?
3. What values do you stand for, even when no one is watching?
4. If you were mentoring someone younger, what values would you want to ignite in them? What "unfinished game" are you still playing?

5. How do shared struggles create lifelong bonds and preserve memory across generations? What role does community play in sustaining legacy?
6. If legacy is a baton passed, what are you doing with what was handed to you? In a world constantly rewriting its rules, how will you leave a lasting mark?

CONCLUSION

As you close these pages, I hope that you see Bobby Grier's story as not just a moment in 1956, but as a timeless call to courage. One man, one game, one choice. That is all it took to show America that unity is possible, even in the face of fatal division.

To Camille and me, this book is more than history. It is an invitation to stand when it would be easier to sit and to believe that your own story has the power to inspire others. Legacy is not built in headlines; it is built in the silent, faithful decisions we make every day.

Thank you for taking this journey with us. By reading and sharing this story, you have become a part of carrying Bobby Grier's legacy forward. And this is only the beginning. Your voice matters. Your story matters. Together, we can keep this movement alive.

THANK YOU FOR READING *NO GRIER, NO GAME*!

To learn more
Scan the QR Code Here:

We appreciate your interest in No Grier, No Game, and value your feedback, as it helps us improve future versions. Please leave your invaluable review on Amazon.com with your feedback. Thank you!